GOLDEN GATE PARK

AN A TO Z ADVENTURE

WRITTEN BY
MARTA LINDSEY

ILLUSTRATIONS BY
MICHAEL WERTZ

WEST MARGIN PRESS

To my 'B is for Beloved' Drew, Helena, and Elise.
And 'T is for Thank You' to everyone who loves and cares for parks! —M.L.

This work is dedicated to my wonderful husband, Andy.
To the Art Gym (Isabel, Marcos, Owen, and Liz). To my sweet Mom.
To Kate, Chris, Sophia, and Eliza. And to my students, who inspire me every day.
Thank you. —M.W.

Text © 2020 by Marta Lindsey
Illustrations © 2020 by Michael Wertz

Edited by Michelle McCann

Library of Congress Cataloging-in-Publication Data

Names: Lindsey, Marta, 1978- author. | Wertz, Michael, illustrator.
Title: Golden Gate Park : an a to z adventure / by Marta Lindsey ;
    illustrated by Michael Wertz.
Description: [Berkeley, California] : West Margin Press, [2020]
    | Audience: Ages 6-8. | Audience: Grades 2-3. | Summary:
    "A whimsical A-to-Z journey through the best sights of
    California's Golden Gate Park"— Provided by publisher.
Identifiers: LCCN 2019046691 (print) | LCCN 2019046692 (ebook) |
    ISBN 9781513263014 (hardback) | ISBN 9781513263021 (ebook)
Subjects: LCSH: Golden Gate Park (San Francisco, Calif.)—
    Juvenile literature. | San Francisco (Calif.)—Juvenile literature.
    | English language—Alphabet—Juvenile literature. | Alphabet
    books—Juvenile literature.
Classification: LCC F869.S37 G645 2020 (print) | LCC F869.S37
    (ebook) | DDC 979.4/61--dc23
LC record available at https://lccn.loc.gov/2019046691
LC ebook record available at https://lccn.loc.gov/2019046692

Proudly distributed by Ingram Publisher Services

Printed in China

24 23 22 21 20 1 2 3 4 5

Published by West Margin Press

WEST
MARGIN
PRESS

WestMarginPress.com

WEST MARGIN PRESS
Publishing Director: Jennifer Newens
Marketing Manager: Angela Zbornik
Editor: Olivia Ngai
Design & Production: Rachel Lopez Metzger

A

IS FOR ARTIST RUTH ASAWA

Paintings hang on walls. Sculptures sit on pedestals. But Ruth Asawa's most famous artwork hangs from the ceiling. You'll find 15 of her wire creations in the de Young Museum—along with lots more awesome art.

B IS FOR BISON

These gigantic beasts (also called buffalo) have lived in the park for more than 100 years. In 1924, 25 sneaky bison escaped in the middle of the night and surprised people living in the nearby Richmond and Sunset neighborhoods.

IS FOR CONCRETE SLIDES

Grab some cardboard and ride the slides! These concrete chutes were built in the 1970s in what's now the Koret Children's Quarter, one of the oldest public playgrounds in America. Add sand for more speed.

D IS FOR DAHLIA

There are so many flowers in the park, it's hard to believe the land was once just a bunch of sand dunes. One of the best flower spots is Dahlia Garden, which bursts with eye-popping blooms of San Francisco's official flower.

E
IS FOR ECOSYSTEMS

From a mountaintop cloud forest
in the Botanical Garden to an underwater
coral reef at the California Academy of Sciences,
you can travel to some of the most extraordinary
ecosystems in the world without ever leaving the park.

F IS FOR FAIRY DOORS

Look for fairy doors in hidden spots throughout the park. Leave something from nature—an acorn or a shiny stone—as a gift for the park's most magical residents.

IS FOR GRIZZLY BEAR

It's true: a famous grizzly bear named Monarch once lived in the park. Monarch tried to escape more than once, but unlike the bison he wasn't successful. He was the model for the bear you see on today's California state flag.

IS FOR HIPPIE HILL

Right on, man! This slope overlooking
Robin Williams Meadow was a popular hangout for
peace-loving people in the 1960s. Stop by today and you
might see drummers, dancers, and even a few tie-dyed shirts.

I

IS FOR INCREDIBLE VIEWS

Want to see the glimmering Pacific, shimmering skyscrapers, *and* the Golden Gate Bridge? Head to the park's best lookouts: Strawberry Hill, the living roof at the California Academy of Sciences, and the Hamon Observation Tower in the de Young Museum.

J IS FOR JAM SESSIONS

From fiddlers at the Hardly Strictly Bluegrass festival to jazz players in the tunnels, some serious jamming happens here. Music has been part of the park since its creation; the Golden Gate Park Band has played here since 1882.

K IS FOR KARL THE FOG

Fog is such a big part of San Francisco that it has a name: Karl. And Karl *loves* the park. When you have a birthday party in the park, Karl often blows out your candles before you can.

L

IS FOR LAWN BOWLING

Decked in white from head to toe, people have been lawn bowling here since 1901. You can still enjoy other sports from Victorian times too, like fly casting and archery.

M IS FOR MONASTERY STONES

William Randolph Hearst had plans for a castle so grand that he shipped thousands of ancient monastery stones from Spain to build it. But he ran out of cash... and his plans crumbled. Today you'll find the stones scattered around the park.

N IS FOR NESTING HERONS

At Stow Lake in spring, look for great blue heron nests (and chicks!) atop the trees of Heron Island. You can see herons in the park year-round, plus red-tailed hawks, Anna's hummingbirds, Steller's jays, red-winged blackbirds, and many others.

IS FOR ORCHID

How many weird and wonderful orchids can you find among the 2,000 plants growing in the Conservatory of Flowers? (Hint: some live in trees.) While you're there, check if the corpse flower is in bloom for a super stinky surprise.

P IS FOR PEDAL BOATS

Want to pretend you're back in time? Head to Stow Lake. Victorian visitors rented boats and did just what we do today: paddle past Huntington Falls, float under the Rustic Bridge, and then dock at the Boathouse.

Q IS FOR QUEEN WILHELMINA GARDEN

When you plant thousands of tulips next to a Dutch windmill, it makes sense to name it after Dutch monarch Queen Wilhelmina. The Murphy Windmill's claim to fame? A local girl once rode one of its sails around 25 times!

R IS FOR ROLLER SKATERS

Imagine going to the park and seeing 20,000 people on roller skates. That was the roller craze of the 1970s. Today you can still find roller skaters and bladers groovin' at a rink next to JFK Drive called Skatin' Place.

S IS FOR SHAKESPEARE GARDEN

Dost thou desire to stop and smell the roses? Then find thy way to this poetic place. 'Tis filled with flowers and plants from Shakespeare's sonnets and plays... look for poppies, pansies, and primroses.

T IS FOR TEA GARDEN

Climb a moon bridge, hop across stepping stones, and watch colorful koi swim by—all at the Japanese Tea Garden. And don't forget to taste a fortune cookie at the Tea House... after all, they were invented here.

U IS FOR UNCLE JOHN'S TREE

Named after John McLaren, who ran the park until he was 96, this majestic Monterey cypress is almost as old as the park itself. Each December it's decorated with lights to become the park's own Christmas tree.

V IS FOR VERDI

Why is the park's giant Giuseppe Verdi statue so hard to find? Because Uncle John *hated* statues. Whenever one was donated to the park, he planted trees and bushes to hide it. Search for all 30 statues, including one of Uncle John himself.

VERDI

W IS FOR WATERFALLS

A trip to the Sierra Nevada mountains gave John McLaren an idea: why not add a waterfall to the park? So they created Huntington Falls on Strawberry Hill. Rainbow Falls was added later. You can hike to the top of both.

X IS FOR X CHIRANTHOMONTODENDRON LENZII

Imagine peeking inside a flower and seeing a monkey's hand waving back at you. Check out this rare blossom with the tongue-twister name—also called the "hybrid monkey hand tree"—in the Botanical Garden. (Say it: kai-ran-tho-mahn-toe-den-dron lens-ee-eye.)

Y IS FOR YACHT CLUB

Ahoy ye landlubbers! Set your sights on Spreckels Lake, where all kinds of miniature vessels—tugboats, sailboats, speedboats, steamboats—sail from March through October. Come cheer on your favorite tiny racer.

Z IS FOR ZEBRA

Gallop off on a red-striped zebra! Charge ahead on an armored unicorn! Fly away on a sharp-toothed sea dragon! You can ride these creatures and more at the historic carousel in the Koret Children's Quarter.

Now we've reached the end of our A to Z adventure.
Ready to go 'round again?

Not long after the Gold Rush, the people of San Francisco decided they needed a great park in order to become a great city. Great idea, right? Golden Gate Park was created in 1870 and is now one of the most visited city parks in the US. I visit it almost every day and wrote this book to share some of the amazing things I've discovered. Have fun exploring!

A Japanese-American artist and activist Ruth Asawa (1926-2013) was known as San Francisco's "sculpture lady." Her work can also be found in the Japanese Tea Garden, left of the entrance.

B Bison were brought to the park in the 1890s along with other zany animal attractions like kangaroos, emus, and moose. At the time, bison were nearly extinct, but the park's breeding program helped bring them back from the brink.

C When the Koret Children's Quarter opened in 1888, it was a newfangled idea to build a place just for kids to play. Back then, children could ride donkeys, buy a snack of buttered bread, and watch performing elephants!

D Dahlias were chosen as the official flower of the city in 1926 because, thanks to their beauty and diversity, they are the "very symbol of San Francisco life and of the spirit of her people." The garden blooms May through November.

E The park is also home to native coastal scrub, dune, and woodland ecosystems. Hike the Phil Arnold Trail to see the old-growth coast live oaks that were saved when the park was created.

F My two favorite spots to find fairy doors are the trees in the Music Concourse and the fallen log across the street from the "Friend Gate" of the Botanical Garden.

G As a publicity stunt for his newspaper, William Randolph Hearst brought California's last wild grizzly bear to San Francisco. Monarch the grizzly lived in the park from 1894 to 1911, at the far western end of what is now the National AIDS Memorial Grove.

H Hippie Hill became a hangout during 1967's Summer of Love. Robin Williams Meadow sits beside it, named in honor of the comedian (1951–2014) who got his start in San Francisco and performed at the park's first Comedy Day.

I Atop Strawberry Hill, look for ruins of an observatory that fell in the 1906 earthquake. The California Academy of Sciences rooftop also has great views, plus native plants growing on it. And the Hamon Observation Tower is a 360-degree must-see!

J Tons of famous musicians have played here, from a legendary show with Jefferson Airplane and the Grateful Dead to Luciano Pavarotti and Marilyn Horne at Opera in the Park. Everyone from Paul McCartney to Metallica have played at Outside Lands, and folk and bluegrass stars jam at Hardly Strictly Bluegrass.

K In 2010, a "mist"-erious account appeared on Twitter for San Francisco's fog called @KarlTheFog. Just like the fog, the name stuck around!

L Parents and older kids can take classes with the San Francisco Lawn Bowling Club and the Golden Gate Angling & Casting Club.

M Good spots to find monastery stones are around Stow Lake, the Japanese Tea Garden, the Botanical Garden, and the National AIDS Memorial Grove. In 1931, Hearst filled 11 ships with stones from Spain's Santa María de Óvila monastery and brought them to America.

N Great blue herons began nesting at Stow Lake in 1993. Each Saturday in spring, volunteers lead Heron Watch walks to look for chicks. The rest of the year you'll find mallards, ring-necked ducks, hooded mergansers, western gulls, buffleheads, and Canadian geese at the lake.

O The Conservatory of Flowers was built in 1879 and is one of the few Victorian buildings still standing in the park today. It's also one of the only remaining wooden conservatories in America.

P Stow Lake and its islands, waterfall, and bridges were completed in the 1890s. Victorian visitors believed the lake was haunted by a woman in a white gown. The story made the front page of the *San Francisco Chronicle* in 1908.

Q The Dutch windmill was built in 1903; its garden was planted and named in 1962 to honor Queen Wilhelmina Helena Pauline Maria. The Murphy windmill was built in 1908, and in 1921 daredevil Velma Tilden did indeed ride it, winning 25 boxes of candy—one for each rotation!

R Visitors have been roller skating in the park since it opened, but the sport got so popular in the 1970s some thought should be banned. Thanks to the efforts of skate legend David Miles Jr., that didn't happen. Instead, the Recreation & Parks Department created a roller rink in 1985.

S The Garden of Shakespeare's Flowers dates back to 1928. Read the Shakespeare quotes on the garden wall and search for more poetic plants like foxlips, lavender, rosemary, and violets.

T The Japanese Tea Garden was created in 1894 by Makoto Hagiwara for California Midwinter Fair. Hagiwara is considered by many to be the inventor of the modern fortune cookie, which he started serving at the Garden's teahouse in the early 1900s.

U It's fitting that a tree is named for John McLaren. During his lifetime he planted 2 million trees at Golden Gate Park and other parks around the city! Each December, a tree-lighting event is held at his tree in front of McLaren Lodge.

V John McLaren took his rather shady approach to statues because he wanted the park to look natural. So today, many statues are easy to miss. Look for opera composer Verdi at the Music Concourse and Uncle John himself in John McLaren Memorial Rhododendron Dell.

W From the top of Huntington Falls, hike along the falls to the stepping stones at the bottom. At nearby Rainbow Falls, you can experience an optical illusion: follow the creek west toward Lloyd Lake and you'll come to a place where it looks like the water flows uphill.

X The monkey hand tree is easy to find in the Botanical Garden's Mesoamerican Cloud Forest. But the hybrid monkey hand tree (featured on the page for "X"), which is crossed with a California chaparral, is nearby but a bit harder to spot.

Y The San Francisco Model Yacht Club was founded in 1898, and Spreckels Lake was built in 1904 for it. If the clubhouse is open, check out their collection of beautiful handmade boats.

Z The carousel you see today arrived in 1941 after being part of the 1939 Golden Gate International Exposition on Treasure Island. Believe it or not, there were once real zebras in the park—they pulled carriages!

ADDITIONAL READING

San Francisco's Golden Gate Park: A Thousand and Seventeen Acres of Stories by Christopher Pollock
Golden Gate Park: San Francisco's Urban Oasis in Vintage Postcards by Christopher Pollock
Karl the Fog: San Francisco's Most Mysterious Resident by Karl the Fog
Map & Guide to Golden Gate Park by Rufus Graphics in Cooperation with San Francisco Recreation & Parks Department
The Trees of Golden Gate Park and San Francisco by Elizabeth McClintock

To explore historic photos of the park, visit opensfhistory.org, foundsf.org, and sfpl.org. For park events and other information, visit sfrecpark.org.

THANK YOU

A special thanks to Christopher Pollock, historian in residence at the San Francisco Recreation and Park Department. His wonderful book, *San Francisco's Golden Gate Park: A Thousand and Seventeen Acres of Stories*, was invaluable to the author's research. He also kindly and carefully fact-checked this book.

MARTA LINDSEY is a writer and park lover. She lives in San Francisco with her family, just one block from Golden Gate Park. Marta's other favorite park is Point Reyes National Seashore, which inspired her first children's book. You can learn more about her at martalindsey.com.

MICHAEL WERTZ is an award-winning illustrator, printmaker, and educator based in Oakland. Known for his playful and vivid imagery, he has collaborated with the de Young Museum, Oakland Museum, and more. You can see more of his work at wertzateria.com.